Contents

INTRODUCTION

Since the Monroe Doctrine, the United States has maintained a substantial interest and influence throughout the Western hemisphere. The United States' concern in Central America drastically increased during the 1980s due to the Marxist coup in Nicaragua and a communist insurgency in El Salvador. After the 1980 election of President Ronald Reagan, a strong anti-communist, the United States' foreign policy in El Salvador was often scrutinized and controversial. In El Salvador, the Reagan administration sought to defeat the communist insurgents, while establishing a democratic government. The Reagan policy of strong political, economic, and military support toward El Salvador assisted in the defeat of the Marxist guerrilla insurgency and allowed for Salvadoran democratic institutions to take root. The United States should utilize these successes and achievements and apply them toward the current U.S. war on terrorism, specifically in the countries of Columbia, the Philippines, and Afghanistan.

In this paper, I will first develop a brief history of El Salvador. Next, I will describe the political situation in El Salvador and its relation to American political assistance during the 1980s war against the Marxist rebels. In the third section, I will analyze El Salvador's economy and American economic aid and show how it supported the counterinsurgency. I will then discuss the military situation in El Salvador and American military support in defeating the Marxist rebels. I will offer some concluding remarks showing how the Reagan policy helped to form a successful outcome to the war against the insurgents. Finally, I will analyze the lessons from the war in El Salvador and apply them to today's war on terrorism.

BACKGROUND

Since about the mid nineteenth century, El Salvador's economy has largely been dependent on its ability to export coffee. This crop and the vast majority of cultivated land was under the control of the Salvadoran elite, a group of Fourteen Families that exploited the Salvadoran people and controlled the country's economy.[1] The elite class reaped its status and benefits at the expense of the lower class by expanding plantations onto the peasant's land and paying them barely enough to survive. This oligarchy of families controlled the banking and mercantile systems, the military and most government positions.[2] With an enormous gap between these two classes, peasant revolt was inevitable. In 1925, Agustin Farabundo Marti began to spread his communist philosophy in El Salvador and fueled peasant unrest.[3] Due to this unrest, the oligarchy made a deal with the military, which allowed military officers to hold public office. In 1931, a military coup ousted the civilian president, allowing the military to rule El Salvador in some form until 1982.[4]

Although the United States began to establish strong financial ties with El Salvador after World War II, American involvement in El Salvador did not significantly increase until the 1960s. Increases in American economic and military aid during the 1960s coincided with the presence of numerous Peace Corp volunteers as well as an increase in American investments.[5] In the 1970s, El Salvador was dependent on American food and American markets for its manufactured goods.[6] From 1974 to 1976, the United States sent an immense amount of military aid but discontinued the aid when Salvadorans were caught selling surplus weapons. Yet by 1978, with leftist forces growing in El Salvador, the Carter administration changed its emphasis

2

away from human rights and towards stopping terror and subversion. By 1980, President Carter reinstated American military aid to El Salvador.[7]

The history of El Salvador consisted of wealth and luxuries for a few and hardship for the masses. The elite class was able to control the economy, the peasants, and the military. Because of its economic and political dominance, virtually no middle class existed; consequently, the differences between the elite and the peasants were extraordinary. The military's rise to power in the twentieth century failed to better the life of Salvadorans. Reforms by every new government never lasted long enough to benefit the peasants. Lacking any legitimate democratic means, the people of El Salvador were starving for the freedoms they eventually received in the 1980s.

POLITCS AND AMERICAN POLITICAL SUPPORT

The political elections of the 1980s were the freest and most democratic El Salvador had ever held. The elections allowed for free participation by multiple political parties, and voter participation in these elections far exceeded previous elections. Prior to the 1980s the rulers of El Salvador obtained power by arranging their own re-election or by taking political control through force.[8] The United States' interest and support in El Salvador helped allow the democratic process take root and grow. Furthermore, the successful implementation of democratic principles helped legitimize the Salvadoran government. This political legitimacy made it easier for the Reagan administration to provide economic and military support for the counterinsurgency. Furthermore, it gave the Salvadoran people a reasonable alternative to following the Marxist rebels.

In October 1979, a five man military junta with support from the United States took control of the government in El Salvador. By the end of the year, the reform goals of these junior officers had failed and they were forced out of office. In January 1980, a new four-man junta rose to power. This new government consisted of an alliance between the military forces and the Christian Democrat political party. Jose Napoleon Duarte was chosen to be the president and head of the junta. He had won the 1972 presidential election but was forced into exile by the military. [9] Duarte's appointment as president broke a string of military rulers in El Salvador and brought some much needed legitimacy to the government. After becoming president in 1980, the Duarte government was placed under tremendous stress from the growing number of Marxist rebels in El Salvador. The insurgents within El Salvador were highly influenced by communist ideology and were financially supported by numerous Communist nations. The overthrow of the Nicaraguan government in 1979 by communist guerrillas was the spark that allowed the insurgents to escalate their communist movement within El Salvador. [10] The Reagan administration believed Duarte's government was the only hope for the transfer of power by democratic means. If it survived, elections would follow. [11]

When Ronald Reagan was elected President of the United States, the Salvadoran rebels threatened to hold their "final offensive" against El Salvador's government. [12] In early January 1981, the rebels began their offensive "promising they would present Reagan with 'an irreversible military situation' by the time he took office." [13] Within three days, the rebel attack was a dismal failure. In a press conference late in the year, President Reagan indicated the lack of overwhelming support for the guerrillas by stating, "the guerrillas have failed miserably in an attempt to bring the population over to their side. The populace is still in support of the government." [14] Through this statement, President Reagan indicated that the United States would continue to support the existing government of El Salvador since, in his opinion; it had the backing of the Salvadoran people.

Early on in his administration, President Reagan and his staff realized the necessity of dealing with El Salvador on a global scale. The Reagan administration was not willing to make the same mistake that was made in Vietnam of failing to pinpoint the source of the problems.[15] In El Salvador, evidence indicated the source of support for the leftist guerrillas came from the Soviet Union and Cuba through Nicaragua. After the rebel offensive had been defeated in 1981, Nicaraguan and Cuban support was fully exposed when many rebel documents and munitions were captured, indicating Soviet involvement.[16] In 1981, the United States also produced evidence from human agents and satellite photography of arms smuggling and of Cuban advisors working with leftist guerrillas. In addition, the United States had evidence the rebels received two thousand captured American weapons and two million rounds of ammunition from Vietnam.[17] In 1982, Soviet style grenade parts and detonators were found, further indicating outside support of the rebels.[18] American concern with Soviet and Cuban involvement in El Salvador was made known to the Soviet Union through diplomatic channels. In 1982, the Reagan administration sent a diplomat to Cuba to discuss the situation in Central America. The United States wanted Cuba to cease its support to El Salvador insurgents, but Castro indicated that this would be difficult to do. In the end, the Reagan administration decided to compete with Cuba on all levels of involvement in Central America.[19] Thus, President Reagan provided direct political support for the Duarte government and its war against the Marxist uprising.

Since Duarte's government survived the rebel insurgency, Constituent Assembly elections were held in March 1982. The Salvadoran turnout for the elections was overwhelming, with over 80% voter participation during the election.[20] The right-wing political parties received

36 Assembly seats, while Duarte's Christian Democrats received 24 seats. The voters clearly dismissed the leftist political parties, which only received eleven percent of the vote.[21] This election showed the people's support for the government as well as its war against the rebels. Thus, the Salvadoran government had no reason to make concessions to the left.

Although the Reagan administration was initially concerned with El Salvador's move to the right and with the right-wing political party National Republican Alliance's (ARENA's) ties with death squads, it was willing to continue to support the legitimately elected government. American concerns lessened when the Salvadoran military used its influence to recommend an independent consensus candidate be chosen as the provisional president.[22] The presidency, although provisional until full elections were held under a constitution, also had great potential power. Thus, it was significant that different political groups jointly decided on a temporary president. Shown from the outcome of this election, Salvadorans chose democracy over authoritarianism and reform over revolt.

Since El Salvador demonstrated positive steps toward a democratic process, the United States strove to support the legitimately elected government in its struggle against the leftist insurgents. United States political support toward El Salvador was essential to Salvadoran success with democracy and in its fight against the insurgents. The Reagan administration was opposed to negotiations with the left concerning division of political power in the Salvadoran government.[23] The new government of El Salvador was in agreement with the United States on this point. El Salvador additionally agreed with the United States that the leftist organizations, the Revolutionary Democratic Front (FDR) and Farabundo Marti National Liberation Front (FMLN)—the military counterpart to the FDR—should be peacefully reintegrated into national life and only obtain political power through the democratic process.[24] However, the rebels did not agree that they could successfully participate in democratic elections and continued to attempt to take power through force and terrorism.

In addition to political support, the United States put political pressure on the Salvadoran government to stop the human rights abuses. Although the death squads of El Salvador occurred throughout its history, they became famous to Americans in 1980 when six Jesuit priests were murdered by an element of the Salvadoran military.[25] By 1982, the deaths attributed to political violence were on a downward trend. The United States put pressure on the newly elected Salvadoran government, which worked hard to control both official violence and the guerrillas. Additionally, the newfound democracy in El Salvador provided alternatives to violence and reconciled opposing political interests.[26] Differences among political factions participating in democracy could now be solved through debate and voting rather than threats and violence.

By the middle of 1983 in El Salvador, the results of the 1982 elections indicated not only success as a process but also success in establishing a functioning, democratic government. The elected Constituent Assembly drafted a new constitution and acted as a legislative body until one was elected under the new constitution. To assist in the elections, the United States sent $3.4 million in aid to help buy computers and other equipment, to acquire technical assistance, and to set up a program for international observers to witness the elections. This American assistance not only benefited the 1984 election but later elections as well by strengthening the institutional electoral process with a minimum of American involvement in the actual administration of the elections.[27]

To further demonstrate United States political support of El Salvador, the rhetoric from President Reagan and his administration clearly showed that Central America and El Salvador were strategically important to the United States. Early in March 1983, Reagan declared that the

Western Hemisphere, including the United States, was endangered by the communist insurgency in El Salvador.[28] Later that month Secretary of State George Shultz stated: "Central America is too close and of too much strategic importance for us to stand idly by…Our security is at stake, and our most basic principles are being tested."[29] In April 1983, during a joint session of Congress, President Reagan again discussed how Central America's problems affected the security of the United States.[30] Through such statements, the Reagan administration not only showed Americans and Salvadorans how critical Central America was to the Untied States, but also made its priorities and intentions known to the Soviet Union, Cuba, and Nicaragua. Furthermore, Reagan's statements expressed not only a strong interest but also a strong ideological support for the Duarte government and its war against the Marxist insurrectionists.

While ways to deal with death squad activities were contemplated, the politics in El Salvador during 1984 centered around the March presidential election. The two leading candidates were Jose Napoleon Duarte of the Christian Democrats and Roberto d'Aubusion of the far-right ARENA. Concern arose in the United States over the possibility of d'Aubusion being elected president. He had extreme right wing political views and had been associated with death squads during the early 1980s. The United States made it obvious prior to the final election that it favored Duarte.[31] Yet, President Reagan indicated America's willingness to support the candidate who won the election: "I believe it is being naïve to express concern for human rights while pursuing policies that lead to the overthrow of less-than perfect democracies by Marxist dictatorships which systematically crush human rights."[32] Thus, Reagan's bottom line was that he would not allow the Marxist rebels to take power even if d'Aubusion won the election.

In May 1984 Salvadorans voted for their nation's first president elected without military intervention in more than 50 years. The confusion about voting procedure that plagued recent elections were absent since the United States worked with Salvadoran officials to establish a more orderly system. Additionally, guerrilla harassment was at a minimum. After all the votes were counted, Duarate won the election by 54% of the vote, enabling him to serve once again as President of El Salvador. The Reagan Administration believed once Duarte was democratically elected, he had the backing of the people and could begin resolving the guerrilla war that had plagued the country for the past four years.[33] Furthermore, this election made President Reagan's request from Congress for economic and military aid to fight the insurgency much easier to obtain.

Shortly after the election, President Reagan addressed United States' interests in Central America during a televised address to the nation. He specifically discussed the need for American support in El Salvador and his belief that Salvadorans wanted democracy and freedom. Reagan further pointed out that even with the terrorist activities of the rebels, "the Government of El Salvador had offered amnesty to the guerrillas and asked them to participate in the elections and democratic process."[34] Yet, the guerrillas refused amnesty, preferring to establish power by military force. Reagan further stated that if these communists could start a war against the people of El Salvador, then Salvadorans and their friends were justified in defending themselves. If the Soviets could aid and abet these insurgencies, then the United States had every right and a moral duty to assist in resisting them.[35] Once again, President Reagan publicly demonstrated his support of Duarte's government and its fight against the insurgency. Reagan's statements gave the newly elected President Duarte assurances that he would continue to receive vital American support.

The legislative elections of 1985 gave Duarte's Christian Democratic party 33 of 60 seats, which allowed Duarte greater ease in enacting his programs into law.[36] Political violence had decreased since Duarte took office and the Salvadoran government continued to receive foreign aid not only from the United States but also from numerous international agencies, parties, and nations.[37] Additionally under Duarte, the army improved, the roots of democracy continued growing, the guerrillas became weaker, and Duarte proceeded to seek a dialog with the rebels. President Duarte continued negotiations with the rebels into 1986 by seeking to end the armed conflict by getting the guerrillas to join party politics. The rebels demanded a negotiated share of power in the government and wanted the government to withdraw its troops from the area surrounding a rebel stronghold.[38] Duarte broke off talks after these demands, signifying that his government would not turn over a part of Salvadoran territory to a group of armed rebels who had no legitimacy.[39] The strong political support of the Reagan administration gave Duarte enough confidence to not concede to the rebels' demands.

On March 22, 1988, legislative and municipal elections were once again held in El Salvador. Duarte's Christian Democrats did not fair well in the election. ARENA won 200 of 262 mayoral posts including San Salvador and won 31 of 60 National Assembly seats. The Christian Democrats controlled only 23 seats.[40] This election was a preview of the 1989 presidential election in which ARENA would also win the Presidency. Salvadorans viewed ARENA's election success more as a punishment toward the Christian Democrats than as an ideological turn to the right. Evidence indicated at least eight cases in which government officials had been involved in corruption. In addition, Salvadorans were concerned that the civil war had not ended and the economy had not gotten significantly better. The United States was concerned about the increased political power of ARENA and its past ties to death squad activities; however, the United States was not willing to end its support. After the elections, Secretary of State George Shultz met with Salvadoran leaders in San Salvador to re-affirm

American commitment to assist in the defeat of the leftist insurgency. In addition, he pressed for the need for continued democracy and avoidance of human right violations.[41]

During President Reagan's two terms in office, the Salvadorans, with American assistance, established strong democratic roots in a nation that had been ruled by the military or the oligarchy for approximately 50 years. The country participated in five national elections in which the people, not the military, elected the candidates. Through these legitimate elections, the Salvadoran government began serious negotiations with the leftist insurgents while attempting to deter right-wing death squads. During this time, the Reagan administration presented El Salvador with continued political support, which helped establish democratic principles in El Salvador and greatly assisted the war against the rebels. Furthermore, it was obvious the people of El Salvador were passionately committed to the democratic rights and liberties they had fought for and won with American support.

THE ECONOMY AND AMERICAN ECONOMIC AID

American economic aid in the 1980s was designed to counter the insurgents' destruction of production and economic infrastructure, to provide emergency assistance to families displaced by the guerrillas, to maintain employment and productivity, and to increase economic growth. With the support of these programs, the Salvadoran government gained additional backing for its counterinsurgency from the people. Also, the United States' economic plan was to reduce inflation and to energize exports, while financing the imports of raw materials and intermediate capital goods to stimulate growth in the private sector and help create jobs.[42] During the 1980s, the Reagan administration sent millions of dollars to El Salvador in economic aid to assist the well-being of the people and to help offset the damage done by the leftist guerrillas. American economic support assisted the Salvadorans in establishing democracy, as well as defending their nation against Marxist rebels.

The Reagan administration had inherited American aid and commitment to El Salvador. In 1980, with the growing Marxist threat in El Salvador, the Carter administration committed $25 million in aid. The Reagan administration continued with these aid packages, with emphasis on economic assistance. In 1981-1983, economic aid to El Salvador was three times the military aid.[43] In addition, the United States established long term trade and investment programs. Beginning in the early 1980s with support from the United States, El Salvador began a program of agrarian reform. Early in 1982, 20% of the land was redistributed, and 60,000 poor farm workers benefited from it. By 1984, 550,000 peasants, or about one quarter of the rural population, was assisted by land reform.[44] One of the rallying points of the Marxist rebels was that the wealthy landowners had taken advantage of the peasants by having them work the land with little pay. The land redistribution program showed the peasants the government was concerned about their welfare and support. Now the peasants received their own land to use and to provide for their family. Thus, this program countered one of the guerrilla's main recruiting points and provided the government with additional support from the people.

Another successful program established with strong urging from the United States combined military involvement with economic rebuilding. This pacification program was formed in 1983 with the help of 15 American military trainers. The program combined aggressive patrolling and night ambushes by the army with the construction of health clinics and schools for villagers.[45] In addition, the American plan moved Salvadorans out of rebel controlled areas into government run relocation camps. Although the government funding for these camps put an additional strain on the Salvadoran economy, and many Salvadorans resented being uprooted from their homes, it enabled the military to more aggressively attack the guerrillas. In the first two and a half months of the pacification program, the Salvadoran government opened 40 schools, enrolled 2,700 new students, opened 12 health clinics and improved more than 40 miles of road. In 1986, another program known as United for Reconstruction was funded by $8 million from the United States. The key to the Reconstruction plan was similar to that of the pacification program, with the Army's effort to draw in private businesses, unions, and the Church as well as civilian ministries to rebuild rural towns after the military cleared them of guerrilla units.[46]

One of the keys to most counterinsurgency programs is providing security to the people. These pacification programs successfully provided security to the rural peasants while allowing the army to more aggressively pursue the guerrillas. Furthermore, these programs fulfilled another key to a successful counterinsurgency by winning the "hearts and minds" of the people. New schools, clinics, and roads brought a higher standard of living to the people. As a result of these programs a majority of Salvadorans continued to support their government and its war against the Marxist rebels.

In a nation ravaged by fighting, United States economic support helped stabilize the Salvadoran economy as much as possible under the existing conditions. As previously indicated, with United States financial and technical assistance hundreds of thousands of acres of land were turned over to the peasants. More than 1,750 primary school classrooms were built for 70,000 children. The availability of drinking water increased dramatically for city dwellers. American funded health programs contributed to the 10% drop in the infant morality rate between 1985 and 1988.[47] By helping stabilize the Salvadoran economy, the United States assisted the

Salvadoran government in its battle against the Marxists, while giving enough stability to allow for democracy to take hold and expand.

MILITARY SITUATION AND AMERICAN MILITARY ASSISTANCE

When President Reagan took office in 1981, the government of El Salvador was engaged in a war against leftist insurgents. When he left office in 1989, the war was still on going; however, it ended in January 1992. These leftist rebels were attempting to take control of El Salvador, which was something President Reagan was determined not to allow. Although President Reagan did not see the ultimate defeat of the rebels during his term, his support of El Salvador stopped the rebel advancement and decreased their numbers and political support. Through American military assistance, El Salvador fought a successful counterinsurgency and stabilized El Salvador's society to hold fair and democratic elections.

As previously mentioned, just prior to President Reagan taking office in January 1981, the Marxist insurgents began their "final offensive" in El Salvador. Similar to other insurgencies throughout history, the rebels believed a conventional defeat of the Salvadoran military would bring them into power. The Salvadoran rebels evolved due to deep anger from decades of dictatorship, which festered among the lower classes and frustrated the emerging middle class.[48] Like the successful insurgency in Nicaragua, the Marxist hoped a general uprising would occur during their offensive actions. In fact, no such event occurred. Essentially no support from the population existed. The rebel initiative was not sustained for more than three days, and the Salvadoran army quickly reestablished control in all parts of the nation.[49]

During the early stages of the conventional engagements, "the guerrillas used highly developed and sophisticated tactics, and were capable of taking on regular El Salvadoran units."[50] Yet, the government forces always had the edge over the guerrillas due to their airpower. Even though the Salvadoran Air Force was small and limited to daytime operations, it still represented the primary firepower of the counterinsurgency. Furthermore, lack of training made it difficult to coordinate with ground forces. Yet, the Salvadoran Air Force performed well in stopping the 1981 offensive.[51] Due to the defeats, the rebels realized their insurgency was not yet prepared for a conventional military victory, and they initiated hit-and-run guerrilla tactics against the Salvadoran industrial infrastructure, trying to bring down the government by destroying the economy. While showing some successes, the FMLN was not able to counter American military aid, nor the ability of Salvadoran military to contain their forces, nor the lack of popular support.[52]

Throughout Ronald Reagan's first year in office, the media and Congress questioned his policies in El Salvador. The greatest concern was direct American troop involvement in El Salvador and the question arose whether El Salvador would become another Vietnam for the United States. The Reagan administration attempted to quell these concerns. The Joint Chiefs of Staff made it known that U.S. troop involvement was not necessary or favored. American military trainers were in El Salvador during 1981 with as many as 30 and as few as 6 personnel.[53] President Reagan, in a press conference in March 1981, tried to reassure the public, declaring, "None of them (U.S. advisors) will be going into combat. None of them will be accompanying El Salvador troops on missions of that kind. They are there for training El Salvador personnel."[54]

Of the military aid sent to El Salvador, almost a quarter was provided to the Salvadoran Air Force. El Salvador had a small army of 10,000 personnel and about 7,000 police in 1980 when the war broke out. What little training the army had was geared toward a conventional war. No training existed for fighting a counterinsurgency campaign. The Salvadoran Air Force consisted of 1,000 men with four flying squadrons and 67 aircraft. The Air Force consisted of 11 outdated attack fighters, 6 C-47 transports, less than 10 trainer aircraft and 13 helicopters.[55] The training in the Air Force was similar to the army as it was geared towards conventional war. The Air Force had only a few pilots and training was only barely adequate.

In the early 1980s, a small group of U.S. military specialists went to the Salvadoran government and military to assist in planning for a war against the rebels. The military strategy was to increase the size of the Salvadoran army and begin training in counterinsurgency operations. The Salvadoran military would also receive modern weapons from the U.S. The use of airpower would play a significant role in the national strategy of the Salvadoran military. The U.S. would assist in modernizing their aircraft and increasing their numbers. Early in 1982, the U.S. delivered four O-2A reconnaissance aircraft, six A-37B counterinsurgency fighters, and two C-123 transports. In addition, improvements with training and weaponry would occur with the U. S. spending $1.4 million on pilot, aircrew, and technical training of Salvadorans in the United States. Since congress had limited the number of American military personnel in El Salvador, the USAF had only five people in country. Thus, the Salvadoran Air Force was trained outside the country and this was accomplished in the U.S. and at Albrook Field in Panama.[56]

In 1982, America was intent on demonstrating to the Soviet Union, Cuba, and Nicaragua American resolve for the government of El Salvador. President Reagan increased the number of American military maneuvers in the region and made plans to hamper the rebel supply lines.[57]

Furthermore, the United States increased military aid and military training to El Salvador. The Reagan administration believed it was getting good value for its aid since the professional performance of the Salvadoran Army was evident in victories against the rebels. More improvements in the military occurred when 1,500 Salvadorans returned home after undergoing military training on counterinsurgency operations in the United States.[58]

The FMLN understood the superiority the Salvadoran Air Force brought to the fight. In addition, the guerrillas understood the aircraft were the most vulnerable when on the ground. The rebel commandos dealt a major blow to the Salvadoran Air Force in January 1982 when they attacked an airbase and destroyed six helicopters, and three aircraft. An additional five aircraft were badly damaged. The raid was well planned and well executed.[59] In addition to attempting to infiltrate airbases, the FMLN established special anti-aircraft units modeled after the Vietnamese. These units tended to set traps for medical evacuation helicopters and gunships. The guerrillas determined the most effective way to take down an aircraft was to catch it in a crossfire. These guerrillas became effective in setting up positions that allowed them to fire on aircraft from several directions. While initially effective, El Salvador's Air Force countered these tactics by placing more medics in the field with units and flying multiple aircraft to provide mutual support when attacking guerrilla forces.[60]

The status of Salvadoran military and its success in 1983 was volatile throughout the year. Starting in February and the early spring, the Salvadoran army endured a number of hardships. The Marxist guerrillas had re-grouped and looked much stronger. In early February, the rebels took over an agriculture town of 30,000 people 70 miles east of San Salvador.[61] The Salvadoran military eventually re-took the town but this incident demonstrated the growing strength of the rebels. By the end of the month, the Salvadoran army was running low on ammunition and spare parts for their combat planes. The Salvadoran government soon requested and received emergency military aid from the United States. This military aid was crucial to the ongoing counterinsurgency. Two months later the military situation improved, without any indications of an imminent victory for the rebels.[62] Even though the Salvadoran military had many hardships in 1982 and early 1983, its ability to counter the rebel advances allowed Salvadorans to participate in democratic elections.

Throughout the summer and fall of 1983, government forces produced a number of successes against the rebels. Secretary of Defense Casper Weinberger visited El Salvador in September and reported that American support and training had helped El Salvador make great progress in their counterinsurgency. Weinberger was impressed with the morale and training of the Salvadoran troops, and he believed their relations with the civilian population were strong.[63] Within a month of Weinberger's visit the rebels were once again on the offensive. The guerrillas were showing signs of better unification, increased intelligence, and more mobility. The rebels had attacked more than 60 towns. AC-47 gunship and UH-1 were used during this time on numerous occasions in support of the Salvadoran military. These airframes were consistent in neutralizing guerrilla advances and supporting government offenses. To further counter the guerrilla's aggressive actions, the Salvadoran military reorganized in November and soon became a more aggressive force.[64]

In January 1984, President Reagan once again supported El Salvador's military by asking Congress to allocate additional military aid and training. In the face of the hit-and-run tactics of the guerrillas, a large portion of the Salvadoran army was being tied down guarding fixed installations. President Reagan wanted to increase the number of troops in order to actively seek out the rebels. He also called for more helicopters to increase the mobility of the troops. After

President Duarte's election, Congress was willing to increase military aid to El Salvador. Obtaining military assistance from the U.S. became easier for El Salvador by holding elections and making advances against the insurgency. Duarte had stated he did not want or need American troops and his military plans were to apply pressure to rebel supply routes, control subversive activity, and keep the rebels off balance.[65] As previously indicated, Duarte also promised to seek negotiations with the rebels. By the end of 1984, El Salvador's armed forces had grown from 9,028 in 1980 to 30,000 troops and were transformed into a modern aggressive fighting machine.[66]

The United States sent the largest amount of military aid during the Reagan years to El Salvador in 1985.[67] This aid was used to increase the numbers, mobility, and effectiveness of the Salvadoran troops. In addition, the Salvadoran Air Force had vastly improved and was ready to take on a larger role against the rebels in air mobility operations and air support. Throughout 1984 and 1985, government forces gained the initiative. "Airpower in the form of A-37 fighters, helicopter gunships, and helicopter lift played a major role in the government's success."[68] During this time, the military had established a small group of well-trained elite units who could be inserted by helicopter to search out the enemy. With effective reconnaissance and use of helicopters, the Salvadoran military could initiate combat on their terms. The U.S. supplied the Salvadoran Air Force with two AC-47 gunships and trained the aircrews to operate the system. The AC-47 soon became one of the most effective weapons in the Salvadoran arsenal.[69] Like successful counterinsurgencies of the past, this superior firepower allowed the government troops to make strategic advances against the rebels. Using a mix of large and small unit operation, the government forces kept the insurgents off balance and on the move. The rebel actions against El Salvador's economy actually hurt their public support. Church leaders, as well as numerous citizens, were now openly denouncing the guerrillas' destruction.[70] Not only were the rebels losing civilian support but also their military forces were steadily decreasing due to the successes of the government. By the end of 1986, the number of rebel forces plummeted to 6,000 from 12,000 in 1984.[71] American military assistance played a vital role in these successes against the insurgents.

By 1988, the Salvadoran military had grown to 43,000 troops, organized into six brigades. In addition, the Air Force grew to 2500 with an airborne battalion, a security group, five airplane squadrons and a large helicopter force. The FMLN conducted a surprise attack in 1989 and obtained some success. One of the main Salvadoran bases was attacked; however, heavy fighting and reinforcements allowed the Salvadoran Air Force to hold the base.[72] Like the major offensive by the guerrillas in 1981, the government forces successfully defeated the insurgents. The military aid, training, and superior firepower obtained from the United States allowed the Salvadoran military to successfully bring a halt to the Marxist insurgency.

Rebel leaders began more serious negotiations to end the armed conflict but the negotiations did not come to fruition before Reagan left office. Yet, President Reagan's military policy and support in El Salvador was pivotal. The Salvadoran government prevented a violent overthrow of its regime by the Marxist insurgents. The number of FMLN decreased over the years, as did their public support. The Salvadoran government, with support from the United States, attempted to negotiate a peaceful settlement. The negotiations failed not because the Salvadoran government offered the rebels to join the democratic process but because the rebels made the unrealistic demand that they automatically be allowed to share political power.

. The insurgents in El Salvador were heavily dependent on Cuba and Nicaragua for weapons and training. The Soviets were also supporters of the guerrilla movement, funneling most of their supplies through Cuba. The fall of the Soviet Union and the end of the Cold War helped to bring about the end to the insurrection in El Salvador. The flow of supplies slowly dried up, as Cuba could no longer afford to support the guerrillas without Soviet support. With the continued successes of the Salvadoran military and the lack of continued military and ideological support from the Soviets and Cubans, the FMLN turned to the United Nations for a resolution to the conflict. By 1992, under a United Nations sponsored settlement, the two sides agreed to terms in which the FMLN did not gain a share of power.[73] Thus, American military assistance contributed to stopping the guerrilla insurgency and allowing democracy to take root.

CONCLUSIONS

In this essay, I have shown that American political, economic, and military support to El Salvador during the Reagan administration was vital to halting the Marxist insurgency and establishing a democratic process. United States support and assistance allowed for five national elections in El Salvador. These elections were the most free and democratic ever held by Salvadorans. The overwhelming involvement in the democratic process of the Salvadoran people demonstrated the inability of the insurgency to gain popular support. Without a mass uprising of the peasants and the working class, the insurgency continuously fought an uphill battle. In successful insurgencies such as Vietnam, the rebels relied heavily on the peasants to provide food, shelter, and safe passage. In El Salvador, the people favored the democratic process over the Marxist ideology. Furthermore, President Reagan stood by the Salvadoran government as he confronted the Soviets and Cubans who were supporting the rebels. To counter the strong Soviet and Cuban ideological support to the rebels, the U.S. provided effective political backing to the Salvadoran government. President Reagan strongly supported the Salvadoran government's refusal to concede any political power to the guerrillas, as well as their attempts to negotiate an end to the war by inviting the rebels to participate in the democratic process. Thus, American guidance in the political process within El Salvador was essential to the Salvadoran government maintaining the support of the people and the ultimate defeat of the insurgency.

American economic aid during the 1980s was essential in winning the hearts and minds of the people and to offset the attacks by the rebels on the economic infrastructure in El Salvador. Additionally, the United States supported two new economic plans: agrarian reform and United for Reconstruction. Both plans benefited the Salvadoran peasants economically and provided them a sense of security. Furthermore, these plans showed the government was concerned about the well-being of the peasants and gave them a legitimate alternative to the rebel cause. The Reagan administration also helped establish long term trading and investment programs between El Salvador and the United States. This economic support provided the Salvadoran government enough stability to successfully continue the counterinsurgency with the support of the people. It is also important to note American economic aid to El Salvador during the 1980s was triple that of the military aid.

Even though El Salvador did not receive as much military as economic aid, military aid was still vital to El Salvador's ability to halt the guerrilla insurgency. The Reagan administration sent essential military supplies and equipment during critical phases of the war, which halted any advances the rebels attempted. Additionally, American training and weaponry played an important role in turning the Salvadoran Army and Air Force into an effective counterinsurgency force. Through military aid and guerrilla warfare training from the United States, the Salvadoran

Army was able to increase in size and effectiveness. American aircraft and flight training contributed greatly to the successes of the Salvadoran Air Force in the counterinsurgency operations. Most importantly to the United States, President Reagan was able to be involved with the military success in El Salvador without sending American combat troops. Thus, with assistance from the United States, the Salvadoran military became an effective counterinsurgency force, allowed democracy to take root, and ultimately defeated the Marxist guerrillas.

President Reagan's foreign policy with El Salvador halted the Marxist insurgents advancement, while helping to establish democratic principles. He understood the Marxist rebels could not bring freedom or prosperity to El Salvador any more than Castro had to Cuba. Deciding to support El Salvador's counterinsurgency, President Reagan was willing to fight for democracy there. By backing the efforts of the Salvadoran people to achieve freedom and prosperity, he was also protecting American security. Many Salvadorans were grateful for American assistance during their counterinsurgency campaign in the 1980s. This attitude was evident in a statement made by President Duarte on October 14, 1987 during a ceremony in his honor in Washington, D.C. Duarte stated, "I've seen through my life many times in which people with hate in their hearts have set fire to the American flag. This time, permit me to go to your flag and, in the name of my people, to give it a kiss."[118] Duarte's gesture showed the Salvadoran's gratitude to the U.S. for its support during their fight against the Marxist rebels.

EPILOGUE

Many lessons from the war in El Salvador are applicable to the current war on terrorism. These lessons apply specifically to smaller conflicts against terrorism such as in Columbia and the Philippines. America must supports both governments as they campaign against the terrorist organizations of the Revolutionary Armed Forces of Columbia (FARC) and Abu Sayyaf. Additionally, some of these lessons are applicable to the current U.S. policy in Afghanistan. The war in El Salvador demonstrated that strong political support, significant economic aid, and extensive military backing over an extended time defeat an insurgency. The United States can implement these policies to defeat terrorist groups in Columbia, the Philippines, and Afghanistan.

Similar to the Reagan administration's political support of the Salvadoran government, the Bush administration must continue to show strong political support for the Columbian, Philippine, and Afghani governments. Supporting continuous free and democratic elections will further legitimize these governments, especially in the new government of Afghanistan. These three governments must show their people that the defeat of terrorist insurgents will bring about lasting democracy and freedom. Of the three countries, Afghanistan most closely resembles El Salvador in meeting the challenges of democracy. Like El Salvador, oppressive leaders have ruled Afghanistan for years. The United States must support Afghanistan as it supported El Salvador by ensuring safe and fair elections are held regularly. If the Afghani people are as committed as the Salvadorans were to the freedom and liberties American support gave them, democracy can successfully take hold in Afghanistan.

President Reagan confronted the governments of Cuba, Nicaragua, and the Soviet Union for their support of the Marxist rebels. President Bush's current war on terrorism also confronts states that sponsor terrorism and terrorist organizations such as Al Qaida who have links to supporting terrorists in the Philippines and Columbia. The Bush administration needs to continue to address terrorism on a global scale. Similar to President Reagan showing the strategic importance of El Salvador, President Bush needs to continue to reiterate the strategic importance of these three nations against the war on terrorism. President Bush must maintain his public support of these countries' fight against the terrorist groups within their nations. President Reagan continuously provided political support to the government of El Salvador, which helped provide stability to the government. Similarly, through continued political support of the leadership in Columbia, the Philippines, and Afghanistan, President Bush helps to legitimize these governments' war on the insurgent terrorist groups.

Economic assistance is another lesson the current administration can use in supporting counterinsurgency programs. Winning the hearts and minds of the citizens of countries fighting an insurgency is critical to a successful outcome. In El Salvador, the U.S. economic aid was substantial and assisted in building new schools, roads, and hospitals for the Salvadoran people. The Bush administration has begun a similar program in the Philippines. New roads and schools are being built by the American military in remote locations where Abu Sayyaf maintains influence. This program should expand into the remote parts of Columbia and needs to play a significant role in the rebuilding of Afghanistan. Similar to the pacification program in El Salvador, the U.S. should train the government military in ways to support the security of the local villages through aggressive patrols of terrorists' strongholds while continuing to construct better infrastructure for these rural communities. Once specific areas are cleared of terrorist organizations, the governments could implement a program like the United for Reconstruction plan in El Salvador. Under this plan, private businesses, unions, and churches assist in further rebuilding local communities. Thus, an aggressive economic plan is essential in supporting the people while routing out the terrorists.

While the Reagan administration successfully pushed for agrarian reform, the Bush administration needs to push for crop reform in Afghanistan and Columbia. Both countries are key contributors to the drug trade. With support from the United States, Afghanistan and Columbia must institute a crop substitution program that will bring steady income to the people. This program must include compensation to the farmers for planting alternative crops. In addition, the U.S. government can support the program by providing seed, irrigation systems, processing techniques, and marketing support. Many parts of Afghanistan and Columbia are fertile and would support the growing of fruits and vegetables. This program could assist in stabilizing the region since terrorist organizations would lose income from the decrease in the illegal drug trade. Furthermore, by planting and harvesting new crops the farmers of these countries could help support their nation and energize the countries' exports. Through strong economic support, the Bush administration can achieve significant in-roads against the war on terrorism.

While lessons can successfully be taken from political and economic support given to El Salvador, the Bush administration can also apply many lessons from military support and training of the Salvadorans. The current administration must realize the long commitment necessary to train military forces to wage a counterinsurgent campaign. The Salvadorans needed three to four years to become an effective fighting force. In addition, Air Forces require an extended time to build infrastructure, train pilots, train maintainers, and coordinate joint operations. As mentioned previously, Congress limited the number of American military personnel in El Salvador. These limits restricted the much-needed training of the Salvadoran military and especially the Air Force. For effective counterinsurgency training in Columbia, the Philippines, and Afghanistan, the U.S. needs to commit to large numbers of trainers and advisors in country.[74]

Many lessons can be taken from the successful counterinsurgency in El Salvador. With American backing, the Salvadoran government forces defeated the insurgents' conventional attacks similar to America's defeat of the conventional forces of Al Qaeda and the Taliban in Afghanistan. Once the conventional phase was completed, the Salvadoran military needed to adapt to the new guerrilla tactics. The Bush administration must allow American military advisors to actively train government forces in counterinsurgency tactics while assisting in planning, coordinating, and implementing raids on terrorist groups. Throughout the war in El Salvador, the guerrillas devised new ways of attacking the government forces. Often, attacks were directed at the Salvadoran Air Force. The Salvadoran Air Force quickly learned the importance of base security after the rebels successfully attacked one of their air bases. This lesson must not be repeated today, and security of air bases must be a top priority. Additionally, the Marxist rebels in El Salvador established new tactics when attacking government medical evacuation helicopters and gunships. To counter such a tactic today, American military trainers can apply the Salvadoran model of placing more medics in the field and flying multiple aircraft for mutual support when attacking terrorist ground forces. The American military must receive support from the Bush administration to provide counterinsurgency training to the Army and Air Force of Columbia, the Philippines, and Afghanistan.

In addition to the training and support for the military, the Bush administration must be willing to send a substantial amount of military aid. This aid can assist these countries in modernizing their weapons and building up of their forces. Through a significant increase in their forces and modernization of their equipment, El Salvador showed they were more successful in countering the insurgents. By increasing the size and capability of their military, these three countries can more aggressively seek out the terrorists, in addition to bringing more security to rural villages.

Since the Air Force played a significant role in defeating the rebels in El Salvador, the U.S. must strongly consider supplying helicopters and modern aircraft to Columbia, the Philippines, and Afghanistan to assist in their war on terrorism. When properly trained, the Salvadoran Air Force showed how a relatively small third world country could play a significant role in stopping an insurgency. Additionally, the Salvadoran Air Force successfully supported the Army throughout the conflict. The O-2 spotter aircraft and AC-47 were used effectively for close support operations, and the A-37 gave the Army a major firepower advantage. UH-1 helicopters supplied by the U.S. were effectively used as troop lift and as medevacs. Both missions were essential for transport in a mountainous country with few roads.[75] While Air Forces are very expensive for a small country to maintain and operate, aircraft with similar capabilities flown by government forces of Columbia, the Philippines, and Afghanistan could result in similar results and assist in defeating terrorist groups in their countries.

Along with sending military support to these governments, the United States must also assist in curbing support to the terrorist groups. As mentioned previously, the insurgents in El Salvador were heavily dependent on Cuba and Nicaragua for weapons and training. The end of the Cold War helped to bring about the end to the insurrection in El Salvador since the flow of supplies slowly dried up, as Cuba could no longer afford to support the guerrillas. Similarly, the United States must work closely with the governments of Columbia, the Philippines and Afghanistan in stopping the flow of arms and money to these terrorist groups. In addition, close coordination needs to occur with other nations bordering these states. Without a constant flow of arms and supplies, these terrorist groups will be much less effective.

While not a perfect model, the war in El Salvador is full of lessons that can be applied to today. Dr. James Corum said it best in his article, "The Air War in El Salvador," that this conflict "as a case study is excellent in that most of the operational and political problems that one is ever likely to face in supporting a nation in a counterinsurgency campaign are all found in El Salvador."[76] President Reagan's military policies and support in El Salvador were crucial in stopping the guerrilla advances and allowing for democracy to take root. If applied on a similar template, President Bush can obtain similar successes in Columbia, the Philippines, and Afghanistan's war on terrorism. While the Monroe Doctrine outlined America's interests in the Western Hemisphere, the attacks of September 11, 2001 and America's war on terrorism outlined America's continued interest on a global scale for the 21st Century.

Notes

[1] Alexander M. Haig Jr., <u>Caveat: Realism, Reagan, and Foreign Policy</u>, (New York: Macmillan Publishing Company, 1984) p. 117.

[2] Walter Lafeber, <u>Inevitable Revolutions: The United States in Central America</u>, (New York: W. W. Norton & Company, 1993) p. 72-73.

[3] Benjamin Keen, <u>A History of Latin America</u>, (Boston: Houghton Mifflin Company, 1992) p. 465.

[4] Keen, p. 466.

[5] Lafeber, pp. 73, 175, 242.

[6] Lafeber, p. 208.

[7] Lafeber, pp. 244-246, 251.

[8] U.S. Dept of State, <u>Certification of Progress in El Salvador</u>, Current Policy No. 410, (Washington, D.C.: Bureau of Public Affairs, 1982) p. 1.

[9] U.S. Congress, House, Committee on Foreign Affairs, <u>Prospects for Peace in El Salvador</u>, 101st Cong., 1st sess., (Washington D.C.: GPO, 1989) pp. 3-4.

[10] Jose Angel Moroni Bracamonte and David E. Spencer, <u>Strategy and Tactics of the Salvadoran FMLN Guerrillas: Last Battle of the Cold War, Blueprint for Future Conflicts</u>, (Westport, Connecticut: Praeger, 1995) p. 3.

[11] Haig, p. 126.

[12] Haig, p. 118.

[13] Christopher Dickey, <u>With the Contras: A Reporter in the Wilds of Nicaragua</u>, (New York: Simon and Schuster, 1985) p. 103.

[14] U.S. President, "Ronald Reagan 1981," <u>Public Papers of the Presidents of the United States</u>, (Washington, D.C.: GPO, 1982) p. 1033.

Notes

[15] Don Oberdorfer, "U.S. Sees Soviets as Key to Solving Salvador Conflict," <u>Washington Post</u>, 14 Jan 1982, p. A1; Bernard Gwertzman, "Problem termed Global," <u>New York Times</u>, 14 Jan 1982, p. 1.

[16] Dickey, p. 104.

[17] Haig, pp. 139-140.

[18] Joanne Omang, "As Salvadoran Politics Boil, U.S. Envoy Shifts Attention," <u>Washington Post</u>, 24 Apr 1982, p. A1.

[19] Haig, p. 136; Dickey, p. 104.

[20] U.S. Dept of State, <u>Central America: Defending Our Vital Interest</u>, Current Policy No. 482, (Washington, D.C.: Bureau of Public Affairs, 1983) p. 2.

[21] U.S. Dept of State, <u>Commitment to Democracy in Central America</u>, Current Policy No. 386, (Washington, D.C.: Bureau of Public Affairs, 1982) p. 1; Lafeber, p. 287.

[22] Omang, p. A22.

[23] Current Policy No. 386, p. 2.

[24] <u>Ibid.</u>

[25] Dickey, p. 87; Bracamonte, p. 35.

[26] Current Policy No. 410, p. 2.

[27] U.S. Dept of State, <u>Elections in El Salvador</u>, Current Policy No. 503, (Washington, D.C.: Bureau of Public Affairs, 1983) p. 3.

[28] George Skelton, "Reagan Sees Salvador Peril," <u>Los Angles Times</u>, 5 Mar 1983, p. 1.

[29] U.S. Dept of State, <u>Strengthening Democracy in Central America</u>, Current Policy No. 468, (Washington, D.C.: Bureau of Public Affairs, 1983) p. 1.

[30] Current Policy No. 482, p. 1.

[31] Linda Chavez, "U.S. Role in Salvador," <u>New York Times</u>, 5 May 1983, p. 6.

[32] Richard Meislin, "Salvador Vote: Rising Fears on Outcome," <u>New York Times</u>, 20 Mar 1984, p. A3.

[33] Bernarnd Gwertzman, "Duarte in Washington, Asserts Salvadoran Army Will Back Him," <u>New York Times</u>, 21 May 1984, p. A1; Richard Meislin, "Salvador Vote For a President; Snags are Minimal," <u>New York Times</u>, 7 May 1984, p. A1.

[34] U.S. Dept of State, <u>U.S. Interests in Central America,</u>, Current Policy No. 576, (Washington, D.C.: Bureau of Public Affairs, 1984) p. 576.

[35] <u>Ibid.</u>

[36] Jose Z. Garcia, "El Salvador: A Glimmer of Hope," <u>Current History</u>, 85 (Dec 1986), p. 411.

[37] U.S. Dept of State, <u>American Foreign Policy Current Documents 1985</u>, Current Policy No. 468, (Washington, D.C.: Bureau of Public Affairs, 1986) p. 1021.

[38] Julia Preston, "Part of El Salvador Finds Peace," <u>Washington Post</u>, 31 Jul 1986, p. A27; U.S. Congress, House, Committee on Foreign Affairs, <u>The Air War and Political Development in El Salvador</u>, 99th Cong., 2nd sess. (Washington D.C.: GPO, 1986), p. 26.

[39] "Salvador Rebels Call Off Peace Talks," <u>Washington Post</u>, 15 Sep 1986, p. A16.

[40] Marjorie Miller, "Salvador Moves to Right as War, Money Woes Continue," <u>Los Angles Times</u>, 28 Mar 1988, p. 14.

[41] Douglas Farah, "Salvadoran Ruling Party Beset From Left, Right as Vote Nears," <u>Washington Post</u>, 17 Mar 1988, p. A37; David B. Ottaway, "Shultz Acts to Reassure Salvadorans," <u>Washington Post</u>, 1 Jul 1988, p. A16.

Notes

[42] American Foreign Policy Current Documents 1987, p. 706; U.S. Dept of State, American Foreign Policy Current Documents 1988, (Washington, D.C.: Bureau of Public Affairs, 1989) p. 726.

[43] Haig, p. 128; U.S. President. "Ronald Reagan 1981," p. 1032.

[44] Current Policy No. 410, pp. 1, 4; Current Policy No. 576, p. 4.

[45] David Wood, "Weinberger in Salvador Battle Zone, Cites Army Gains Against Rebels," Los Angeles Times, 8 Sep 1983, p. 5.

[46] Keen, p. 474; Wood, p. 5; Preston, p. A28.

[47] U.S. Dept of State, American Foreign Policy Current Documents 1989, p. 711.

[48] James LeMoyne, "El Salvador's Forgoten War," Foreign Affairs, 68 (Summer 1989) p. 118.

[49] U.S. Congress, House, Committee on Foreign Affairs, U.S. Policy Options in El Salvador, 97th Cong., 1st sess., (Washington D.C.: GPO, 1981) p. 3.

[50] Bracamonte, p 66.

[51] James S. Corum, " The Air War in El Salvador," Aerospace Power Journal, Summer 1998, p. 5.

[52] U.S. President. "Ronald Reagan 1981," p. 1033; Bracamonte, p. 39.

[53] Haig, p. 128; U.S. Congress, House, Committee on Foreign Affairs, U.S. Policy Options in El Salvador, p. 4.

[54] U.S. President. "Ronald Reagan 1981," p. 206.

[55] Corum, pp. 1-3.

[56] Corum, pp. 4-5.

[57] Oberdorfer, p. A18.

[58] Current Policy No. 386, p. 1-2.

[59] Corum, p. 5.

[60] Bracamonte, pp. 141-142, 149.

[61] Keen, p. 472; "Salvador units Head for City Held by Rebels," Los Angeles Times, 2 Feb 1983, p. 8.

[62] David Wood, "Salvador Army Asks U.S. for Emergency Aid," Los Angeles Times, 18 Feb 1983, p. 6; Leslie H. Gelb, "State Dept Aides Said to Question Acts in Nicaragua," New York Times, 7 Apr 1983, p. A16.

[63] Wood, "Weinberger," p. 5.

[64] Linda Chavez, "Salvador Rebels Make Gains and U.S. Advisors are Glum," New York Times, 4 Nov 1983, p.1; Joachim H.Maitre, "The Dying War in El Salvador," Strategic Review, Winter 1985, p. 129; Bracamonte, p. 108.

[65] Hedrick Smith, "Reagan Planning More Aid for Salvador," New York Times, 4 Jan1984, p. A3.

[66] Dario Moreno, U.S. Policy in Central America: The Endless Debate, (Miami: Florida International University Press, 1990) p. 121. Maitre, p.126.

[67] Moreno, p. 121.

[68] Corum, p. 6.

[69] Ibid.

[70] U.S. Congress, House, Committee on Foreign Affairs, The Air War and Political Development in El Salvador, p. 31; Hose Z. Garcia, "Democratic Consolidation in El Salvador," Current History, 87 (Dec 1988), p. 422.

Notes

[71] Garcia, "A Glimmer of Hope," p. 409.

[72] Corum, pp. 8-9.

[73] U.S. President, "Ronald Reagan 1987," <u>Public Papers of the Presidents of the United States,</u> (Washington, D.C.: GPO, 1988) p. 1177; LaFeber, p. 358.

[74] Corum, pp. 10-11.

[75] Corum, p. 14.

[76] Corum, p. 15.

BIBLIOGRAPHY

PRIMARY SOURCES

BOOKS

Bracamonte, Jose Angel Moroni and David E. Spencer, <u>Strategy and Tactics of the Salvadoran FMLN Guerrillas: Last Battle of the Cold War, Blueprint for Future Conflicts</u>, Westport, Connecticut: Praeger, 1995.

Dickey, Christopher, <u>With the Contras: A Reporter in the Wilds of Nicaragua</u>, New York: Simon and Schuster, 1985.

Haig, Alexander M. Jr., <u>Caveat: Realism, Reagan, and Foreign Policy</u>, New York: Macmillan Publishing Company, 1984.

GOVERNMENT DOCUMENTS

U.S. Congress, House, Committee on Foreign Affairs, <u>The Air War and Political Development in El Salvador</u>, 99th Cong., 2nd sess. Washington D.C.: GPO, 1986.

U.S. Congress, House, Committee on Foreign Affairs, <u>Prospects for Peace in El Salvador</u>, 101st Cong., 1st sess., Washington D.C.: GPO, 1989.

U.S. Congress, House, Committee on Foreign Affairs, <u>U.S. Policy Options in El Salvador</u>, 97th Cong., 1st sess., Washington D.C.: GPO, 1981.

U.S. Dept of State, <u>American Foreign Policy Current Documents 1985</u>, Washington, D.C.: Bureau of Public Affairs, 1986.

U.S. Dept of State, <u>American Foreign Policy Current Documents 1987</u>, Washington, D.C.: Bureau of Public Affairs, 1988.

U.S. Dept of State, <u>American Foreign Policy Current Documents 1988</u>, Washington, D.C.: Bureau of Public Affairs, 1989.

U.S. Dept of State, <u>American Foreign Policy Current Documents 1989</u>, Washington, D.C.: Bureau of Public Affairs, 1990.

U.S. Dept of State, <u>Central America: Defending Our Vital Interest</u>, Current Policy No. 482, Washington, D.C.: Bureau of Public Affairs, 1983.

U.S. Dept of State, <u>Certification of Progress in El Salvador</u>, Current Policy No. 410, Washington, D.C.: Bureau of Public Affairs, 1982.

U.S. Dept of State, <u>Commitment to Democracy in Central America</u>, Current Policy No. 386, Washington, D.C.: Bureau of Public Affairs, 1982.

U.S. Dept of State, <u>Elections in El Salvador</u>, Current Policy No. 503, Washington, D.C.: Bureau of Public Affairs, 1983.

U.S. Dept of State, <u>Strengthening Democracy in Central America</u>, Current Policy No. 468, Washington, D.C.: Bureau of Public Affairs, 1983.

U.S. Dept of State, <u>U.S. Interests in Central America,</u>, Current Policy No. 576, Washington, D.C.: Bureau of Public Affairs, 1984.

U.S. President, "Ronald Reagan 1981," <u>Public Papers of the Presidents of the United States,</u> Washington, D.C.: GPO, 1982.

U.S. President, "Ronald Reagan 1987," <u>Public Papers of the Presidents of the United States,</u> Washington, D.C.: GPO, 1988.

NEWSPAPERS

Chavez, Linda, "Salvador Rebels Make Gains and U.S. Advisors are Glum," <u>New York Times</u>, 4 Nov 1983, p.1.

Chavez, Linda, "U.S. Role in Salvador," <u>New York Times</u>, 5 May 1983, p. 6.

Farah, Douglas, "Salvadoran Ruling Party Beset From Left, Right as Vote Nears," <u>Washington Post</u>, 17 Mar 1988, p. A37.

Gelb, Leslie H., "State Dept Aides Said to Question Acts in Nicaragua," <u>New York Times</u>, 7 Apr 1983, p. A16.

Gwertzman, Bernarnd, "Duarte in Washington, Asserts Salvadoran Army Will Back Him," <u>New York Times</u>, 21 May 1984, p. A1.

Gwertzman, Bernard, "Problem termed Global," <u>New York Times</u>, 14 Jan 1982, p. 1.

Meislin, Richard, "Salvador Vote For a President; Snags are Minimal," <u>New York Times</u>, 7 May 1984, p. A1.

Meislin, Richard, "Salvador Vote: Rising Fears on Outcome," <u>New York Times</u>, 20 Mar 1984, p. A3.

Miller, Marjorie, "Salvador Moves to Right as War, Money Woes Continue," <u>Los Angles Times</u>, 28 Mar 1988, p. 14.

Oberdorfer, Don, "U.S. Sees Soviets as Key to Solving Salvador Conflict," <u>Washington Post</u>, 14 Jan 1982, p. A1;

Omang, Joanne, "As Salvadoran Politics Boil, U.S. Envoy Shifts Attention," <u>Washington Post</u>, 24 Apr 1982, p. A1.

Ottaway, David B., "Shultz Acts to Reassure Salvadorans," <u>Washington Post</u>, 1 Jul 1988, p. A16.

Preston, Julia, "Part of El Salvador Finds Peace," <u>Washington Post</u>, 31 Jul 1986, p. A27;

"Salvador Rebels Call Off Peace Talks," <u>Washington Post</u>, 15 Sep 1986, p. A16.

"Salvador Units Head for City Held by Rebels," <u>Los Angeles Times</u>, 2 Feb 1983, p. 8.

Skelton, George, "Reagan Sees Salvador Peril," <u>Los Angles Times</u>, 5 Mar 1983, p. 1.

Smith, Hedrick, "Reagan Planning More Aid for Salvador," <u>New York Times</u>, 4 Jan1984, p. A3.

Wood, David, "Salvador Army Asks U.S. for Emergency Aid," <u>Los Angeles Times</u>, 18 Feb 1983, p. 6;

Wood, David, "Weinberger in Salvador Battle Zone, Cites Army Gains Against Rebels," <u>Los Angeles Times</u>, 8 Sep 1983, p. 5.

SECONDARY SOURCES

BOOKS

Keen, Benjamin, <u>A History of Latin America</u>, Boston: Houghton Mifflin Company, 1992.

Lafeber, Walter, <u>Inevitable Revolutions: The United States in Central America</u>, New York: W. W. Norton & Company, 1993.

Moreno, Dario, <u>U.S. Policy in Central America: The Endless Debate</u>, Miami: Florida International University Press, 1990.

JOURNALS

Corum, James S., " The Air War in El Salvador," <u>Aerospace Power Journal</u>, Summer 1998, p. 5.

Garcia, Jose Z., "Democratic Consolidation in El Salvador," <u>Current History</u>, 87 (Dec 1988), p. 421-424.

Garcia, Jose Z., "El Salvador: A Glimmer of Hope," <u>Current History</u>, 85 (Dec 1986), p. 409-412.

LeMoyne, James, "El Salvador's Forgoten War," <u>Foreign Affairs</u>, 68 (Summer 1989) p. 105-125.

Maitre, Joachim H., "The Dying War in El Salvador," <u>Strategic Review</u>, Winter 1985, p. 129;